Mo Lyn –

What can I
say – I thought of
you! Because of His Love –

Christie

S0-AAC-411

Quiet Moments with Patrick
and the Celtic Saints

Quiet Moments with Patrick
AND THE Celtic Saints

120 DAILY READINGS

Selected by June Skinner Sawyers

CHARIS

SERVANT PUBLICATIONS
ANN ARBOR, MICHIGAN

© 1999 by Servant Publications
All rights reserved.

Charis Books is an imprint of Servant Publications especially designed to serve
Roman Catholics.

Published by Servant Publications
P.O. Box 8617
Ann Arbor, Michigan 48107

Cover design: Left Coast Design, Portland, Oregon
Cover illustration: Archive Photos, New York, NY. Used by permission

99 00 01 10 9 8 7 6 5 4 3 2 1

Printed in the United States of America
ISBN 1-56955-137-5

Cataloging-in-Publication Data on file at the Library of Congress.

Introduction

Celtic spirituality is enjoying a late twentieth-century revival. Indeed, one could say that interest in the spiritual traditions of the ancient Celts is at an all-time high. The Celtic notion of making the commonplace special and the special commonplace strikes a resonant chord among modern seekers. For in the Celtic worldview, the sacred and the profane, the pagan and the Christian, the visible and the invisible, lived side by side. Every living—and nonliving—thing was somehow connected, since the ancient Celts believed that God resided everywhere, in everyone, in everything. The wisdom of the Celtic saints, monks, and mystics represented Christianity at its most humble, in its purest form.

The Celtic church flourished roughly from the fifth to twelfth centuries, with the sixth century in particular considered the zenith of Celtic monasticism. Monasteries at such places as Kildare, Clonard, Clonfert, Glendalough, and Clonmacnoise in Ireland, and Iona and Whithorn in Scotland, to name but a few, served as important centers of learning and pilgrimage as well as social outposts of hospitality, charity, and goodwill. Behind the monastery walls, pilgrims found refuge and a sense of inner peace.

Particular characteristics are

often attributed to Celtic Christianity. An ascetic lifestyle was highly valued—the early Celtic saints were greatly influenced by the desert fathers—as was a love of silence and solitude. Consequently, the Celts felt a strong affinity for remote, solitary places. Perhaps living on the edge of the known world exacerbated their sense of isolation. At the same time, a profoundly restless spirit gripped a goodly number of Celtic saints, an almost uncontrollable urge that found full expression in the various pilgrimages they set out on, the most famous being the St. Brendan Voyage.

The vast majority of Celtic saints remained mystics at heart, feeling most at home surrounded, on the one hand, by the silence within their humble dwellings and, on the other, by the vastness of nature, yet finding reassurance in knowing that they were loved by an all-embracing God. It is this deep and abiding faith that rings through the centuries and is, perhaps, the early Celts' greatest legacy. It is this quality too—this absolute devotion to something greater than themselves—that many people today find so attractive. Through their ancient writings we can almost glimpse the eternal.

Most of the following selections and excerpts capture the simple faith of a profoundly spiritual people. Some passages are very short—thoughts for the day or age-old nuggets expressed succinctly in a sentence or two—others are longer. A considerable number are strikingly poetic, almost visionary in theme and execution. The selections are either written by the saints themselves, attributed to the saints, inspired by the saints, or composed by disciples of the saints. Do take the time to savor the prayers, rules, hymns, and poems of an ancient people whose hard-earned wisdom and practical common sense find remarkable currency for us today.

I Arise Today

Christ with me, Christ before me, Christ behind me,
Christ in me, Christ beneath me, Christ above me,
Christ on my right, Christ on my left,
Christ when I lie down, Christ when I sit down,
Christ when I arise,
Christ in the heart of every man who thinks of me,
Christ in the mouth of every one who speaks of me,
Christ in every eye that sees me,
Christ in every ear that hears me.

—St. Patrick

Saint Ninian of Whithorn (c. 360-432)

St. Ninian had a profound influence on southwestern Scotland. Born the son of a British king and educated in Rome, Ninian converted the pagan Picts in Scotland to Christianity in 397. The church that he founded, the Candida Casa, or White House, in Whithorn, was an important place of pilgrimage throughout the Middle Ages.

TWO

I Will Seek the Truth

I have sought in mine own land Him whom my soul loveth. I sought Him, but I have found Him not. I will arise now, and I will compass sea and land. I will seek the truth which my soul loveth.

—from *Lives of St. Ninian and St. Kentigern*

Saint Patrick
(c. 390-461)

Although not the first missionary to reach Ireland, St. Patrick is credited with converting the pagan population to Christianity. The son of a Roman official, Patrick was captured by raiders and spent many years in slavery in Ireland. Eventually he escaped and returned to his family. In 432 he returned to Ireland and began his campaign of conversion. He is Ireland's patron saint and undoubtedly the most famous of all the Celtic saints.

The Spirit of St. Patrick

Christ above us, Christ beneath us,
Christ beside us, Christ within us.
Invisible we see you, Christ above us.
With earthly eyes we see above us,
clouds or sunshine, grey or bright.

But with the eye of faith
we know you reign,
instinct in the sun ray,
speaking in the storm,
warming and moving all creation,
Christ above us....

Invisible we see you, Christ beneath us.
With earthly eyes we see beneath us

stones and dust and dross....
But with the eyes of faith,
we know you uphold....

Inapprehensible we know you, Christ beside us.
With earthly eyes we see men and women,
exuberant or dull, tall or small.
But with the eye of faith,
we know you dwell in each....

Intangible, we touch you, Christ within us.
With earthly eyes we see ourselves,
dust of the dust, earth of the earth....

Christ above us, beneath us,
beside us, within us,
what need have we for temples made with hands?

—George MacLeod,
inspired by "St. Patrick's Breastplate"

I Am Patrick, a Sinner

I am Patrick, yes a sinner and indeed untaught; yet I am established here in Ireland where I profess myself bishop.

I am certain in my heart that "all that I am" I have received from God.

—from *The Confession of St. Patrick*

FIVE

One Must Know Oneself

Even if I am imperfect in so many ways,
nonetheless I want my brothers and my family to know
my mettle,
so that they may clearly recognize the set of my soul.

—from *The Confession of St. Patrick*

In His Mercy
He Lifted Me Up

I began life more rustic than any man
you care to name:
an exile, unschooled—that much is plain—
a man, what's more, "who does not even know how to
make out for his future";
yet I am sure in my mind of one thing:
that before I was brought low,
I was like some great stone lying deep in mud,
until "He who is power" came
and "in his mercy" lifted me up.

—from *The Confession of St. Patrick*

The Love of God Grows Within Me

More and more the love of God and fear of him grew
strong within me,
and as my faith grew, so the Spirit became more and more
active,
so that in a single day I would say as many as a hundred
prayers,
and at night only slightly less.
Although I might be staying in a forest or out on a
mountainside,
it would be the same;
even before dawn broke, I would be aroused to pray.
In snow, in frost, in rain,
I would hardly notice any discomfort,
and I was never slack but always full of energy.

—from *The Confession of St. Patrick*

EIGHT

I Give Thanks to My God

I am never weary of giving thanks to my God,

who has kept me safe "in the day of my trial."

In such a way that today I may in full confidence offer him a
    sacrifice

of my soul as "a living victim" to Christ my Lord.

For it is he who "has defended me from all my afflictions,"

so that I may say to him, "Who am I, Lord,"

or what is my calling,

that you have appeared to me in such divine power.

So that today, among the gentiles,

I may praise you ceaselessly

and magnify your name,

wherever I may be.

And this, not merely in good times,

but also in distress.

So that whatever will come my way,

whether good or bad,

I may accept it calmly,

and always give thanks to God,

who has shown me

how I should believe in him unfailing without end.

—from *The Confession of St. Patrick*

I Await His Promise

And there I want to "await his promise,"
for he never deceives,
as he promises in the gospel:
"They shall come from the east and from the west
and they will sit down at table with Abraham and Isaac and
    Jacob";
just as we believe that the faithful will come from the
whole world.

—from *The Confession of St. Patrick*

TEN

It Is Our Duty

It is our duty to fish well and with loving care,
just as the Lord urges and teaches us:
"Come after me, and I will make you fishers of men."

—from *The Confession of St. Patrick*

he Will Shield Me

And he will shield me from every evil,
so that I do no sin in his sight.

—from *The Confession of St. Patrick*

He Who Knows All Things

Let him who wants mock me and jeer,
I shall not be silent. For I may not conceal those signs and
  wonders
which the Lord has shown me
many years before they even come to pass,
for he is who knows all things even "before the world began."

—from *The Confession of St. Patrick*

I Am Lifted Up Beyond All Measure

Yet I am aware, even "in this present world,"
how I am lifted up beyond all measure.
I myself was not worthy nor
do I deserve that he should ever treat me in such a way.
For I know full well
that poverty and adversity would suit me better than riches
  and delights.
Yet "Christ the Lord was poor for our sake";
and I myself am but a wretched failure,
having nothing to my name, even had I wanted worldly
  goods.

—from *The Confession of St. Patrick*

FOURTEEN

He Will Fill Your Every Need

As the prophet says: "Throw your thought on God alone and he will fill your every need."

—from *The Confession of St. Patrick*

FIFTEEN

I Commend My Soul to God

Mark it now, "I commend my soul to my God who is utterly
    faithful,"
for whom, in spite of my obscurity, I act as an ambassador.
Yet since he sees through any falsehood in man,
he himself chose me for this task,
to be one of the least among his servants.

—from *The Confession of St. Patrick*

We Who Adore Christ

We who believe and adore the true sun that is Christ,
who will never die,
nor "will those who have done his will"
but "abide forever, just as Christ himself will abide for all
    eternity";
who reigns with God the Father all-powerful,
and with the Holy Spirit before time began,
and now and through all ages of ages. Amen.

—from *The Confession of St. Patrick*

Patrick's Vow

But I beg and beseech all those who believe and fear God,

whoever comes across this writing and takes the trouble to read
  it through,

namely the writing of Patrick, a sinner who, though he was
  never taught,

wrote it down in Ireland,

that no man ever say, if in my ignorance I have accomplished
  any small thing, however trivial,

or if I have shown the way according to God's good purpose,

that this was my own ignorance at work:

but rather, know and believe it to be the undeniable truth that it
  was the gift of God.

This is my Confession before I come to die.

—from *The Confession of St. Patrick*

To Saint Patrick

O Patrick in the Paradise
Of God on high,
Who lookest on the poor man
With a gracious eye,
See me come before thee
Who am weak and bare,
O help me into Paradise
To find thee there.

— Patrick O'Donnell
from *Celtic Christian Spirituality*

Patrick's Blessing on Munster

God's blessing upon Munster,
Men, women, children!
A blessing on the land
Which gives them fruit!

A blessing on every wealth
Which is brought forth on their marches!
No one to be in want of help:
God's blessing upon Munster!

A blessing on their peaks,
On their bare flagstones,
A blessing on their glens,
A blessing on their ridges!

Like sand of sea under ships
Be the number of their hearths:
On slopes, on plains,
On mountain-sides, on peaks.

Kuno Meyer

TWENTY

Profession of Faith in the Trinity

There is no God, nor was there ever in the past nor will there be in the future, except God the Father ingenerate, without beginning, from whom all beginning flows, who controls all things, as our formula runs: and his Son Jesus Christ whom we profess to have existed with the Father, begotten spiritually before the origin of the world in an inexpressible way by the Father before all beginning, and through him were made things both visible and invisible....

—from *Patrick in His Own Words*

Prayer of Thanksgiving

I give thanks to my God tirelessly who kept me faithful in the day of trial, so that today I offer sacrifice to him confidently, the living sacrifice of my life to Christ, my Lord, who preserved me in all my troubles. I can say therefore: Who am I, Lord, and what is my calling that you should cooperate with me with such divine power? … We are indeed witnesses that the Good News has been preached in distant parts, in places beyond which no man lives.

—from *St. Patrick's Confession*

TWENTY-TWO

Prayer for Perseverance

I now entrust my soul to God, who is most faithful and for whom I am an ambassador in my humble station. For God has no favorites and he chose me for this office to become one of his ministers, even if among the least of them.

—from *St. Patrick's Confession*

An Even-Song

May Thy holy angels, O Christ, son of living God,
Guard our sleep, our rest, our shining bed.

Let them reveal true visions to us in our sleep,
O high-prince of the universe, O great king of the mysteries!

May no demons, no ill, no calamity or terrifying dreams
Disturb our rest, our willing, prompt repose.

May our watch be holy, our work, our task,
Our sleep, our rest without let, without break.

—Kuno Meyer

TWENTY-FOUR

He Comes With Shaven Crown

He comes, he comes, with shaven crown, from off the storm-
    toss'd sea,
His garment pierced at the neck, with crook-like staff comes he,
Far in his house, at its east end, his cups and patens lie,
His people answer to his voice. Amen, Amen, they cry.
Amen, Amen.

—from *The Literature of the Celts*

Saint Brigid
(c. 457-525)

Probably the most beloved of Ireland's female saints, St. Brigid was known for her generosity toward the poor and has often been called "Mary of the Gaels," as much for her graciousness as her piety. Brigid founded a convent for both men and women at Kildare and continued the missionary work begun by Patrick. She is also the patron saint of animals.

Brigid's Prayer

Brigid, defend me,
Mary, defend me,
Michael, defend me,
By land and by sea.

—from *Carmina Gadelica*

Brigid and Her Cross

Cross, Cross, Brigid and her Cross,
Mary and her Son,
Brigid and her Cloak,
Good as we are today
May we be seven times better
a year from now.

—Traditional

TWENTY-SEVEN

Brigid's Advice

Fill your hamper and God
will put somewhat therein.

—from *The Martyrology of Oengus the Culdee*

TWENTY-EIGHT

Brigid's Wish

For everything that Brigid would ask of the Lord was granted her at once. For this was her desire: to satisfy the poor, to expel every hardship, to spare every miserable man.

—from *The Martyrology of Oengus the Culdee*

Feast of the Bride

Feast of the Bride, feast of the maiden.
Melodious Bride of the fair palms.

Thou Bride fair charming,
Pleasant to me the breath of thy mouth,
When I would go among strangers
Thou thyself wert the hearer of my tale.

—from *Carmina Gadelica*

Feast Day of Bride

As far as the wind shall enter the door
On the Feast Day of Bride,
The snow shall enter the door
On the Feast Day of Patrick.

—from *Carmina Gadelica*

Bride the Aid-Woman

There came to me assistance,
Mary fair and Bride;
As Anna bore Mary,
As Mary bore Christ,
As Eile bore John the Baptist
Without flaw in him,
Aid thou me in mine unbearing,
Aid me, O Bride!

—from *Carmina Gadelica*

Kindling the Fire

I will raise the hearth-fire
As Mary would.
The encirclement of Bride and of Mary
On the fire, and on the floor,
And on the household all.

—from *Carmina Gadelica*

THIRTY-THREE

Abide in Christ

May I abide in Christ.
May the brightness he gave Brigid lie on me.
May the delight he gave Brigid lie on me.
May the blossom he gave Brigid lie on me.
May the calmness he gave Brigid lie on me.

—from *The Soul of Celtic Spirituality:
In the Lives of Its Saints*

Saint Brendan
(c. 486-575)

St. Brendan was born near Tralee, in County Kerry. One of the most beloved of Irish saints, he established numerous monasteries in Ireland. The most famous is in Clonfert, which became one of the greatest and most durable of Irish monastic schools. Brendan is best known for his love of travel. The Brendan Voyage lasted seven years and may have taken the saint and his disciple monks to Iceland, Greenland, and even as far away as America.

THIRTY-FOUR

The Lord Is Just in All His Ways

The Lord is just in all his ways and holy in all his works.
For he has revealed to his servants such great wonders.

—from *The Voyage of Saint Brendan*

God, Who Knows the Unknown

God, who knows the unknown and reveals all that is secret,
you know the distress of my heart. I implore your majesty
to have pity and reveal to me, a sinner, through your great
mercy your secret that I now look upon with my eyes. I rely
not on what I deserve or my worth, but rather on your boundless pity.

—from *The Voyage of Saint Brendan*

Seeking the Land of Promise

Seven years in all were they
On the voyage—fair was the band—
Seeking the land of promise
With its flocks, a strong subtle turn.

And they found it at last
In the high meads of the ocean,
An island rich, ever lasting, undivided,
Abounding in salmon, fair and beauteous.

—from *Lives of Irish Saints*

I Beseech the Father

I beseech the Father, through the Son; I beseech the Son, through the Father; I beseech the Holy Spirit, through the Father and the Son, and through every creature that praiseth the Lord, that all vice may be removed far from me, and that every saintly virtue may take root in my heart and soul.

—from *Brendaniana*

THIRTY-EIGHT

I Bear Witness Before the King

I bear witness before the King of the stars that the things of this world are no more to me than sand of the sea or leaves of the wood.

—from *Lives of Irish Saints*

The Prayer

We were alone on the wide watery waste—
Nought broke its bright monotony of blue,
Save where the breeze the flying billows chased,
Or where the clouds their purple shadows threw.
We were alone—the pilgrims of the sea—
One boundless azure desert round us spread;
No hope, no trust, no strength, except in thee,
Father, who once the pilgrim people led....

We breathed aloud the Christian's filial prayer,
Which makes us brothers even with the Lord;
Our Father, cried we, in the midnight air adored;
In heaven and earth, be thy great name
May thy bright kingdom, where the angels are,
Replace this fleeting world, so dark and dim.

And then, with eyes fixed on some glorious star
We sang the Virgin-Mother's vesper hymn! ...

'Twas thus in hymns and prayers and holy psalms,
Day tracking day, and night succeeding night,
Now driven by tempests, now delayed by calms,
Along the sea we winged our varied flight.

—*Brendaniana*

Saint Ciaran of Clonmacnoise (c. 512-545)

Born in County Roscommon, St. Ciaran of Clonmacnoise was the son of a carpenter. He founded the famous monastery at Clonmacnoise, one of the truly great learning centers of medieval Europe, about 545. Ciaran was a disciple of Enda of Aran and Finian of Clonard, two influential saints in the Celtic church.

A Multitude of Mercies

"According to the multitude of your mercies, cleanse my iniquity"
(Psalm 51).

> O star-like sun,
> O guiding light,
> O home of the planets,
> O fiery-maned and marvellous one,
> O fertile, undulating, fiery sea,
> Forgive.
>
> O fiery glow
> O fiery flame of Judgment,
> Forgive.

O holy story-teller, holy scholar,
O full of holy grace, of holy strength,
O overflowing, loving, silent one,
O generous and thunderous giver of gifts,
Forgive.

O rock-like warrior of a hundred hosts,
O fair-crowned one, victorious, skilled in battle,
Forgive.

—from *Celtic Christian Spirituality*

Pray With Me to God

O dear brothers, pray with me to God that I may not go to him alone, but that I may take others with me; and that my way to the King may not be a dark way, and that He may give me welcome.

—from *Lives of Irish Saints*

Passing to Heaven

It may be that you will have passed on to heaven before you really appreciate its full value. Better therefore that you suffer its loss that it may benefit another.

—from *The Celtic Monk*

Heaven's Reward

Heaven is the reward of the person who, for the sake of all people, disciplines his own heart.

—from *The Celtic Monk*

Saint Comghall of Bangor (c. 517-602)

St. Comghall of Bangor established a monastery in Bangor, County Down. Among his disciples were Columbanus, Gall, and Moluag.

To Love Christ

In this lies the heart of the rule: to love Christ, to shun wealth, to remain close to the heavenly King, and to be gentle toward all people.

—from *The Celtic Monk*

The Three Rules of Comghall

These three following counsels should be your guide, and nothing should be allowed to separate you from them: namely, have forbearance, humility, and the love of God in your heart.

—from *The Celtic Monk*

Do Not Lament

Do not lament should even great calamities be your lot.
These trials are outnumbered by those suffered by the King
who sends them.

—from *The Celtic Monk*

Saint Columba
(c. 521-597)

Born at Gartan, in County Donegal, of royal blood, St. Columba, also known as Columcille, established his first monastery at Derry in 548. He also founded the monastery of Durrow in County Offaly. In 563 he sailed with his twelve followers to establish a monastery on Iona, off the west coast of Scotland, allegedly choosing exile as an act of penance for a transgression he had committed back home. From Iona, he spread Christianity throughout Scotland and northern England.

St. Columba in Iona

Delightful would it be to me
On a pinnacle of rock,
That I might often see
The face of the ocean;
That I might watch its heaving waves
Over the wide sea
When they chant music to their Father
Upon the world's course;
That I might see its level sparkling strand,
It would be no cause of sorrow;
That I might hear the song of the wonderful birds,
Source of happiness;
That I might hear the thunder of the clamorous waves
Upon the rocks;

That I might hear the roar by the side of the church
Of the surrounding sea ...
That I might bless the Lord
Who orders all;
That I might search in all the books
That which would help my soul;
At times kneeling to the heaven of my heart,
At times singing psalms....

—from *The Poem Book of the Gael*

St. Columba's Plant

I will pluck what I meet,
As in communion with my saint,
To stop the wiles of wily men,
And the arts of foolish women.

—from *Carmina Gadelica*

Altus Prosator

The Most High, planning the frame and harmony of the world,
had made heaven and earth, had fashioned the sea and the waters,
and also shoots of grass, the little trees of the woods,
the sun, the moon and the stars, fire and necessary things,
birds, fish and cattle, beasts and living creatures,
and finally the first-formed man, to rule with prophecy.

At once, when the stars were made, lights of the firmament,
the angels praised for His wonderful creating
the Lord of this immense mass, the Craftsman of the Heavens.
With a praiseworthy proclamation, fitting and unchanging,
in an excellent symphony they gave thanks to the Lord,
not by any endowment of nature, but out of love and choice....

By the singing of hymns eagerly ringing out,
by thousands of angels rejoicing in holy dances,
and by the four living creatures full of eyes,
with the twenty-four joyful elders
casting their crowns under the feet of the Lamb of God,
the Trinity is praised in eternal threefold exchanges.

—from *Iona: The Earliest Poetry of a Celtic Monastery*

FIFTY

The High Creator

The High Creator, Ancient of Days and Unbegotten
was without origin of beginning and without end;
He is and shall be to infinite ages of ages
with Whom is Christ the only begotten
and the Holy Spirit,
coeternal in the everlasting glory of the Godhead.
We set forth not three gods,
but we say there is One God,
saving our faith in three most glorious persons.

—from *Irish Liber Hymnorum*

Columba's Wort

Soothing and salving
With the wort of Columba,
Soothing and salving
With the grace of the God of life.

—from *Carmina Gadelica*

Adiutor laborantium

O helper of workers,
ruler of all the good,
guard on the ramparts
and defender of the faithful,
who lift up the lowly
and crush the proud,
ruler of the faithful,
enemy of the impenitent,
judge of all judges,
who punish those who err,
pure life of the living,
light and Father of lights,
shining with great light,
denying to none of the hopeful
your strength and help,
I beg that me, a little man
trembling and most wretched,
rowing through the infinite
    storm
of this age,
Christ may draw after Him to
    the lofty
most beautiful haven of life
… an unending
holy hymn forever.
From the envy of enemies you
    lead me
into the joy of paradise.
Through you, Christ Jesus,
who live and reign …

—from *Iona: The Earliest*
Poetry of a Celtic Monastery

Noli Pater

Father, do not allow thunder and lightning,
lest we be shattered by its fear and its fire.

We fear you, the terrible one, believing there is none like you.
All songs praise you throughout the host of angels.

Let the summits of heaven, too, praise you with roaming lightning,
O most loving Jesus, O righteous King of Kings.

Blessed for ever, ruling in right government,
is John before the Lord, till now in his mother's womb,
filled with the grace of God in place of wine or strong drink.

Elizabeth of Zechariah begot a great man:
John the Baptist, the forerunner of the Lord.

The flame of God's love dwells in my heart
as a jewel of gold is placed in a silver dish.

—from *Iona: The Earliest Poetry*
of a Celtic Monastery

Alone With Thee, My God

Alone with none but thee, my God,
I journey on my way;
What need I fear, when thou art near,
O King of night and day?
More safe am I within thy hand,
Than if a host did round me stand.

My destined time is fixed by thee,
And Death doth know his hour.
Did warriors strong around me throng,
They could not stay his power;
No walls of stone can man defend
When thou thy messenger dost send.

My life I yield to thy decree,
And bow to thy control
In peaceful calm, for from thine arm
No power can wrest my soul....

The child of God can fear no ill,
His chosen dread no foe;
We leave our fate with thee, and wait
Thy bidding when to go.
'Tis not from chance our comfort springs,
Thou art our trust, O King of Kings.

—from *In Search of Columba*

Iona of My Heart

Iona of my heart,
Iona of my love,
Instead of monks' voices
Shall be lowing of cattle;
But ere the world come to an end,
Iona shall be as it was.

—Traditional

Amra Choluimb Chille
(THE ELEGY OF COLUMCILLE)

Great God, protect me
from the fiery wall,
the long trench of tears.
Just God, truly near,
who hears my wailing
from cloudy heaven.

By the grace of God Colum rose
   to exalted companionship;
awaiting bright signs, he kept
   watch while he lived.
His lifetime was short,
scant portions filled him.

He was learning's pillar in every
   stronghold,
he was foremost at the book of
   complex Law.
The northern land shone,
the western people blazed,
he lit up the east
with chaste clerics.
Good the legacy of God's angel
when he glorified him.

—from *Iona: The Earliest
Poetry of a Celtic Monastery*

Columcille, the Scribe

For weariness my hand writes ill,
My small, sharp quill runs rough and slow;
Its slender beak with failing craft
Puts forth its draught of dark, blue flow.

And yet God's blessed wisdom gleams
And streams beneath my fair-brown palm
The while quick jets of holly ink
The letters link of prayer or psalm.

So, still my dripping pen is fain
To cross the plain of parchment white,
Unceasing at some rich man's call,
Till wearied all am I to-night.

—from *The Book of Irish Poetry*

FIFTY-EIGHT

Derry

This is why I love Derry:
For its level fields, for its brightness,
For the hosts of its white angels,
From one end to the other.

—from *Betha Colaim Chille: Life of Columcille*

Shepherd of Monks

Shepherd of monks, judge of clerics, finer than things,
than kingly gates, than sounds of plaques, than battalions....

He possessed books, renounced fully claims of kingship:
for love of learning, he gave up wars, gave up strongholds.

—Beccan mac Luigdech* from *Iona:*
The Earliest Poetry of a Celtic Monastery

*An Irish hermit associated with the Iona community

Bound to Columba

Bound to Columba, while I speak,
may the bright one guard me in the seven heavens;
when I go to the road of fear,
I'm not lordless: I have strength.

—Beccan mac Luigdech from *Iona:*
The Earliest Poetry of a Celtic Monastery

He Served With a Blessed Hand

He served with a blessed hand,
he often spent nights withdrawn;
silence, too, thinness of side;
Britain's beacon, his mouth's wisdom.

—Beccan mac Luigdech from *Iona:
The Earliest Poetry of a Celtic Monastery*

Behold Iona!

Behold Iona!
A blessing on each eye that seeth it!
He who does a good for others
Here, will find his own redoubled
Many-fold!

—Traditional

The Christian Life

What is best for the Christian life? Simplicity and single-mindedness. A careless Christianity which resists great bother, its trial in fire will be great, its reward in heaven will be small. An active Christianity which resists great comfort, its trial in fire will be small, its reward in heaven will be great.

What is best for the mind? Breadth and humility, for every good thing finds room in a broad, humble mind. What is worst for the mind? Narrowness and closedness, and constrictedness, for nothing good finds room in a narrow, restricted mind.

—The Alphabet of Devotion* from
Iona: The Earliest Poetry of a Celtic Monastery

* The Alphabet of Devotion *is said to have been written by Colman mac Beognae, a pupil of Columba.*

The Right Way to Truth

Should there be anyone who seeks truth, it is necessary for him that he really understand what hides it and what discloses it. Truth hides itself from those who despise it and shows itself to all who go all the way with it.

—The Alphabet of Devotion from *The Celtic Monk*

SIXTY-FIVE

Devotion

What best serves devotion? Simplicity and sincerity.

—The Alphabet of Devotion from *The Celtic Monk*

What Is Best for the Soul?

What is best for the soul? Humility and magnanimity, since all food finds room in an ample humble mind.

—The Alphabet of Devotion from *The Celtic Monk*

The Commandments

Anyone wishing to observe the commandments should follow the path in which all travel; that is to say, charity, humility, and patience must be taken to heart. In this way the commandments will not be lost and he will have possession of them whole and entire.

—The Alphabet of Devotion from *The Celtic Monk*

Who Is Closest to God?

Who is closest to God? The person who contemplates him.
Whom does God aid? The person who does good.

—The Alphabet of Devotion from *The Celtic Monk*

The Love of God

What does the love of God do to a person? It kills his desires. It purifies his heart. It protects him. It banishes vices. It incurs rewards. It lengthens life. It cleanses the soul.

—The Alphabet of Devotion from
Iona: The Earliest Poetry of a Celtic Monastery

On the Desire for Truth

If there is anyone who desires the truth, it is fitting that he have proper knowledge of what conceals it and what reveals it. The truth conceals itself from everyone who slights it. It reveals itself to everyone who fulfills it.

—The Alphabet of Devotion from
Iona: The Earliest Poetry of a Celtic Monastery

On the Virtues of the Soul

When is a person able to testify to the souls of others? When he can testify to his own soul first. When is he capable of correcting others? When he can correct himself first.

—The Alphabet of Devotion from
Iona: The Earliest Poetry of a Celtic Monastery

A Light in the Dark

As a lantern raises its light in a dark house, so truth rises in the midst of faith in a person's heart.

—The Alphabet of Devotion from
Iona: The Earliest Poetry of a Celtic Monastery

What Is Wisdom?

Wisdom which has no learning is preferable
to learning without wisdom.

—The Alphabet of Devotion from *The Celtic Monk*

SEVENTY-FOUR

Good Deeds

Good deeds flow from love and holy deeds lead to
the eternal life of heaven.

—The Alphabet of Devotion from *The Celtic Monk*

The Struggle

Shame on my thoughts, how they stray from me!

I fear great danger from this on the Day of Eternal Judgment.

During the psalms they wander on a path that is not right;

they run, they distract, they misbehave before the eyes of the great God....

One moment they follow ways of loveliness, and the next ways of riotous shame—no lie! ...

O beloved truly chaste Christ, to whom every eye is clear, may the grace of the sevenfold

Spirit come to keep them, to hold them in check!

Rule this heart of mine, O swift God of the elements,

that you may be my love, and that I may do your will!

—Traditional

SEVENTY-SIX

Peace

O God, grant us thy peace,
the peace of men also,
the peace of St. Columba, the kind,
and of St. Mary mild, the loving one,
and of Christ, the King of human hearts.

—Traditional

The Rule of Columcille

Take not of food till thou art hungry.
Sleep not till thou feelest desire.
Speak not except on business.

—Traditional

From Erin's Shores

From Erin's shores Columba came
To preach and teach and heal,
And found a church which showed the world
How God on earth was real.

In greening grass and reckless wave,
In cloud and ripening corn,
The Celtic Christians traced the course
Of grace through nature borne.

In hosting strangers, healing pain,
In tireless works for peace,
They served the servant Christ their Lord
And found their faith increase.

In simple prayer and alien land,
As summoned by the Son,
They celebrated how God's call
Made work and worship one.

God grant that what Columba sowed
May harvest yet more seed,
As we engage both flesh and faith
To marry word and deed.

—inspired by Columba from *Love From Below*

SEVENTY-NINE

Lord, You Are My Island

Lord, you are my island; in your bosom I rest.

You are the calm of the sea; in that peace I stay.

You are the deep waves of the shining ocean.

With their eternal sound I sing.

You are the song of the birds; in that tune is my joy.

You are the smooth white strand of the shore; in you is no gloom.

You are the breaking of the waves on the shore; your praise is
echoed in the swell.

You are the Lord of my life; in you I live.

—from *The Soul of Celtic Spirituality:*
In the Lives of Its Saints

Prayer of St. Columba

Kindle in our hearts, O God,
The flame of that love which never ceases,
That it may burn in us giving light to others.
May we shine forever in your holy temple,
Set on fire with your eternal light,
Even your Son Jesus Christ,
Our Savior and Redeemer.

—from *The Soul of Celtic Spirituality:*
In the Lives of Its Saints

I Long to Be in the Heart of an Island

I long to be in the heart of an island,
on a rocky peak, to look out often upon
the smooth surface of the sea.

To see the great waves on glittering
ocean ceaselessly chanting music to
their Father.

To watch the murmur of little waves
against the rocks, to listen to the
sea-sound, like keening by a graveyard.

To watch across the watery sea its
splendid bird-flocks, to behold—greater
than any wonder—its monstrous whales.

To see the changing course of ebb
and flood; and this to be my name—
I tell a secret thing—"He who
turned his back on Ireland."

—from *The Music of What Happens*

EIGHTY-TWO

Devotion

Cherish every practice of devotion greatly.

—from *The Celtic Monk*

EIGHTY-THREE

Forgiveness

Forgive every person from your heart.

—from *The Celtic Monk*

The Faithful Departed

Be very constant in your prayers for the faithful departed, as if each dead person were a personal friend of yours.

—from *The Celtic Monk*

For the Love of God

Love God with all your heart and with all your strength.

—from *The Celtic Monk*

EIGHTY-SIX

Columba's Farewell

Beloved children, I charge you, since I am departing
from you, to have perfect love one for another in
whatsoever place ye be in.

—from *Betha Colaim Chille: Life of Columcille*

Great Was His Wisdom

Columcille on whom was no trouble,
Great his wisdom, good his understanding;
A falsehood never passed his lips,
And never did he do vanity.

—Dallan Forgaill*
from *Betha Colaim Chille: Life of Columcille*

*Dallan Forgaill was an Irish poet and a contemporary of Columba.

EIGHTY-EIGHT

Columba's Legacy

While he spoke the wind was silent.

> —from *The Legends and Commemorative*
> *Celebrations of St. Kentigern,*
> *His Friends, and Disciples*

Saint
Columbanus
(c. 543-615)

Born in County Leinster, St. Columbanus performed extensive missionary work on the European continent, establishing numerous monasteries throughout Europe. The best known was at Luxeuil. A strict diciplinarian, Columbanus practiced an austere and rigorous lifestyle.

Understanding the Creator

If you want to understand the Creator
seek to understand created things.

—Traditional

O Lord, Work Good in Me

O Lord God, destroy and root out whatever the Adversary plants in me, that with my sins destroyed you may sow understanding and good work in my mouth and heart; so that in act and in truth I may serve only you and know how to fulfil the commandments of Christ and to seek yourself. Give me memory, give me love, give me chastity, give me faith, give me all things which you know belong to the profit of my soul. O Lord, work good in me, and provide me with what you know that I need. Amen.

—from *Celtic Christian Spirituality*

From Birth to Death

I am always moving from the day of birth
until the day of death.

—from *Columbanus in His Own Words*

NINETY-TWO

Pilgrims

Since we are travelers and pilgrims in the world, let us ever ponder on the end of the road, that is our life, for the end of our roadway is our home.

—from *Columbanus in His Own Words*

NINETY-THREE

Be Helpful

Be helpful when you are at the bottom of the ladder and be the lowest when you are in authority. Be simple in faith but well trained in manners; demanding in your own affairs but unconcerned in those of others. Be guileless in friendship, astute in the face of deceit, tough in time of ease, tender in hard times....

—from *Columbanus in His Own Words*

Be Pleasant

Be pleasant when things are unpleasant, and sorrowful when they are pleasant. Disagree where necessary, but be in agreement about truth. Be serious in pleasures but kindly when things are bitter....

—from *Columbanus in His Own Words*

Be Submissive to Good

Be submissive to good, unbending to evil, gentle in generosity, untiring in love, just in all things. Be respectful to the worthy, merciful to the poor.

—from *Columbanus in His Own Words*

On Faith

Who then is God? He is Father, Son, and Holy Spirit, yet one God. Seek no further concerning God; for those who wish to know the great deep must first study the nature of things. Knowledge of the Trinity is properly compared to the depth of the sea, according to that saying of the Sage: "And the great deep, who shall discover it?" If then a man wishes to know the deepest ocean of divine understanding, let him first, if he is able, scan that visible sea. The less he finds his knowledge to be of those creatures which lurk beneath the sea, the more he should realize his ignorance of the depths of his Creator.

—from *Columbanus in His Own Words*

On Human Life

Oh human life, fragile and mortal. How many have you deceived! How many have you inveigled! How many have you blinded! Though you fly, you are nothing. Though you are seen, you are but a shadow. Though you arise, you are only smoke. Daily you depart and daily you commence. When you are coming, you are going, and when you are going, you are coming, unequal at the end, alike at the beginning, unequal in pleasure, alike in passing away; sweet to the stupid, bitter to the wise. Those who love you don't know you, and those who despise you really understand you. Therefore you are not true but false. You display yourself as true; you prove yourself false.

—from *Columbanus in His Own Words*

The Road to Life

What then are you, human life? You are the road of mortals and not their life, with sin at the beginning and death at the end.... So you are the road to life, not life itself; you are a real road but not a level one, long for some, short for others, broad for some, narrow for others, joyful for some, sad for others, for all alike fleeting and irrevocable. A road is what you are, a road; but you are not clear to all. Many see you, and few understand you to be a road.

—from *Columbanus in His Own Words*

Our True Homeland

Let us now seek en route what shall be in our homeland. Therefore we must beware lest perhaps we be carefree on the way, and fail to reach our true homeland.

—from *Columbanus in His Own Words*

On Remorse

Lord, grant me, I pray you, in the name of Jesus Christ, your Son, my God, the charity that does not fail, so that my lamp may always be lighted, never extinguished, and may burn for me and give light to others…. May I love and contemplate you alone and may my lamp ever burn and shine before you.

I beseech you, most loving Savior, show yourself to us who seek you, so that knowing you we may love you as warmly in return— may love you alone, desire you alone, contemplate you alone by day and night and keep you always in our thoughts.

—from *Columbanus in His Own Words*

Life's Seasons

In countless ways life's seasons disappear,
They all pass by, the months complete a year,
With every moment, tottering age draws near.

Into eternal life that you may go,
Spurn now the sweet deceits of life below,
Soft lust can upright virtue overthrow.

—from *Columbanus in His Own Words*

Carmen Navale*

Lo, little bark on twin-horned Rhine
From forests hewn to skim the brine,
Heave, lads, and let the echoes ring;

The tempests howl, the storms dismay,
But manly strength can win the day,
Heave, lads, and let the echoes ring.

For clouds and squalls will soon pass on,
And victory lie with work well done,
Heave, lads, and let the echoes ring.

Hold fast! and all is well,
God sent you worse, he'll calm this swell,
Heave, lads, and let the echoes ring.

So Satan acts to tire the brain,
And by temptation souls are slain,
Think, lads, of Christ and echo him.

Stand firm in mind 'gainst Satan's guile,
Protect yourselves with virtue's foil,
Think, lads, of Christ and echo him.

Strong faith and zeal will victory gain,
The old foe breaks his lance in vain,
Think, lads, of Christ and echo him.

The King of virtues vowed a prize
For him who wins, for him who tries,
Think, lads, of Christ and echo him.

—from *Columbanus in His Own Words*

Columbanus' most famous poem, said to have been written by the saint in 610 while traveling up the Rhine with a boat full of fellow monks.

how the Monk Should Please God

What is the best thing in the world? To please its Creator. What is his will? To fulfill what he commanded, that is, to live justly and devotedly to seek the eternal; for devotion and justice are the will of God who is himself devout and just. How do we reach this goal? By application. Then we must apply ourselves in devotion and justice. What helps to sustain this? Understanding which, while it winnows the remainder and finds nothing solid to remain in amongst those things which the world possesses, turns in wisdom to the one thing which is eternal. For the world will pass, and daily passes, and revolves towards its end (for what does it have to which it does not assign an end?) and somehow it is supported upon the pillars of vanity. But when vanity comes to an end, then it will fall and will not stand.

—from *Celtic Christian Spirituality*

The Lord Is Our Fountain of Life

The Lord himself, our God Jesus Christ, is the fountain of life, and so he calls us to himself, the fountain, that we may drink of him. He who loves drinks of him, he drinks who is filled with the word of God, who loves enough, who desires enough, he drinks who burns with the love of wisdom.

—from *Celtic Christian Spirituality*

The Thirst, the Hunger

If you thirst, drink the fountain of life; if you hunger, eat the bread of life; blessed are they who hunger for this bread and thirst for this fountain; though they are always eating and drinking, they still long to eat and drink.

—from *Celtic Christian Spirituality*

Creator of Light

The Author of life is the fountain of life, the Creator of light, the fountain of glory. Therefore, spurning the things that are seen, journeying through the world, let us seek the fountain of glory, the fountain of life, the fountain of living water, in the upper regions of the heavens, like rational and most wise fishes, that there we may drink the living water which springs up to eternal life.

—from *Celtic Christian Spirituality*

Saint Kentigern
(d. 612)

St. Kentigern founded a monastery at Glasgow and was consecrated a bishop there. Affectionately known as St. Mungo, he is Glasgow's patron saint and is buried in Glasgow Cathedral. His name lives on in other ways. The St. Mungo Museum of Religious Life, reportedly the only museum of its kind in the world, is located across from the cathedral.

St. Kentigern's Flight Into the Desert

Emulating the fervor of Elias and John the Baptist, and of the Savior himself, he retired to desert places every Lent, and so by withdrawing himself in flight from the sight of the sons of men, and remaining in a solitude of body and soul, he dwelt with himself.

—from *Lives of St. Ninian and St. Kentigern*

Beware Hypocrisy

Beware, dearest ones, of the vice of hypocrisy, which in a way is the renunciation of faith, the abandonment of hope, the emptying of charity,... the blinding of truth.

—from *Lives of St. Ninian and St. Kentigern*

Hail, Festive Season

Hail, festive season, famed in story,
When, of St. Kentigern, the glory
Is wafted to the highest heaven,
While his pure dust to earth is given.

—from *The Legends and Commemorative Celebrations
of St. Kentigern, His Friends, and Disciples*

God's Glory

God's glory, St. Mungo, and smile ever bright,
Have clothed thee in robes of celestial light.

—from *The Legends and Commemorative
Celebrations of St. Kentigern,
His Friends, and Disciples*

Saint Kevin of Glendalough (d. 618)

St. Kevin of Glendalough was born in the sixth century in County Leinster. Kevin, who is also known as Coemgen, founded the influential monastic city of Glendalough and remains one of Ireland's most popular saints. He is known for his patience.

St. Kevin's Hymn to St. Patrick

On a certain night, St. Kevin and his monks were engaged singing a hymn to St. Patrick. Suddenly, the holy abbot remained in silent ecstasy and then ordered his brothers to sing this hymn three times. When the monks asked why they should sing it so often, the abbot said, "Our holy patron Patrick, whose hymn you have sung, stood on the pavement, leaning on his staff and he blessed us, when we ceased our singing."

—John O'Hanlon, from *Lives of the Irish Saints*

Kevin's Prayer

Coemgen crossed the summits
With the angel—'twas great swiftness—
He built a monastery among the glens;
The heavenly Father blessed it from above.

—from *Lives of the Irish Saints*

The Blood of His Hands

Alas! a pain greater than the requital
My hand like a log under the blackbird;
The blood of his hands, of his side, of his feet
The King of heaven shed for my sake.

—from *Lives of the Irish Saints*

Saint Carthage
(d. 639)

St. Carthage, also known as Mochuta, was born in County Kerry. He founded a monastery in County Offaly, where he served as abbot for some forty years. He died in Lismore in 639.

The Rule of Carthage

Whatever good you desire from everyone, do you likewise toward all, that you may reach the kingdom of heaven.

—from *The Celtic Monk*

Saint Aidan
(d. 651)

S t. Aidan was the first bishop and abbot of
Lindisfarne, a small island off the coast of
northern England. Guided by his humility and gentle
nature, Lindisfarne became the cradle of Christianity
in northern England. In the island's churchyard
stands a statue of the saint, crozier in one hand and a
torch in the other.

St. Aidan's Island

Lord, this bare island, make it thy place of peace.
Here be the peace of brothers serving men.
Here be the peace of holy rules obeying.
Here be the peace of praise by dark or day.
Be this island thy holy island.
I, Lord, thy servant Aidan, speak this prayer.
Be it in thy care. Amen.

—Traditional

Forgive Us for Being Proud

Lord, Aidan was humble and lowly; forgive us for being proud.
Lord, have mercy. Lord, have mercy.
Lord, Aidan was patient; forgive us for being impatient.
Christ, have mercy. Christ, have mercy.
Lord, Aidan witnessed with constant love; forgive us for being inconsistent.
Lord, have mercy. Lord, have mercy.

O God, your gentle apostle Aidan befriended everyone he met.
Grant us the same humble, Spirit-filled zeal, that we may inspire others to learn your ways, and thus pass on the torch of faith.
Amen.

—from *The Soul of Celtic Spirituality:
In the Lives of Its Saints*

Saint Cuthbert
(c. 634-687)

Most beloved saint of Northumbria, St. Cuthbert
was a monk and bishop of Lindisfarne in
northern England. Born in southern Scotland, in 651
he joined a monastery in Melrose before living the life
of a hermit on the island of Farne. Against his wishes,
he was made bishop of nearby Lindisfarne. After
many years ministering to the needs of his people,
he returned to his beloved Farne, where he died.

Shepherd of Thy People

Almighty God,
who didst call thy servant Cuthbert from keeping sheep
to follow thy Son and to be a shepherd of thy people,
mercifully grant that we,
following his example and caring for those who are lost,
may bring them home to thy fold,
through thy Son Jesus Christ our Lord.
Amen.

—Traditional

Saint Cuthbert

When once a winter storm upon the shores of Fife
Drove Cuthbert; in despair, one fearful comrade saith:
"To land in such a storm is certain loss of life!"
"Return," another cried, "by sea is equal death."
Then Cuthbert, "Earth and sea against us both are set,
But friends, look up, for Heaven lies open to us yet."

—from *The Book of Irish Poetry*

The Deer's Cry
(OR, ST. PATRICK'S BREASTPLATE)

I arise to-day
Through a mighty strength, the invocation of the Trinity,
Through belief in the threeness,
Through confession of the oneness
Of the Creator of Creation.

I arise to-day
Through the strength of Christ's birth with his baptism,
Through the strength of his crucifixion with his burial,
Through the strength of his resurrection with his ascension,
Through the strength of his descent for the judgment of Doom.

I arise to-day
Through the strength of heaven:
Light of sun,
Radiance of moon,
Splendor of fire,
Speed of lightning.
Swiftness of wind,
Depth of sea,
Stability of earth,
Firmness of rock.

I arise to-day
Through God's strength to pilot me:
God's might to uphold me,
God's wisdom to guide me,
God's eye to look before me,
God's ear to hear me,
God's word to speak for me,
God's hand to guard me,

God's way to lie before me,
God's shield to protect me,
God's host to save me
From snares of devils,
From temptations of vices,
From every one who shall wish me ill,
Afar and anear,
Alone and in a multitude.

I arise to-day
Through a mighty strength, the invocation of the Trinity,
Through belief in the threeness,
Through confession of the oneness
Of the Creator of Creation.

—Kuno Meyer

Celtic Rune of Hospitality

I saw a stranger yesterday;
I put food in the eating place,
drink in the drinking place,
music in the listening place;
and in the sacred name of the Triune God
he blessed myself and my house,
my cattle and my dear ones,
and the lark said in her song
often, often, often,
goes the Christ in a stranger's guise.

—Traditional

ACKNOWLEDGMENTS

3. From *The Whole Earth Shall Cry Glory* by the Rev. George F. MacLeod. Wild Goose Publications/The Iona Community, Glasgow, 1985. Used by permission.

4–17. From *The Confession of Saint Patrick*, translated by John Skinner. © 1998 by John Skinner. Used by permission of Doubleday, a division of Random House, Inc.

18. From *Celtic Christian Spirituality: An Anthology of Medieval and Modern Sources* by Oliver Davies and Fiona Bowie. © 1995 by Oliver Davies and Fiona Bowie. Reprinted by permission of The Continuum Publishing Company. See also readings 40, 90, and 103-6.

20–22. From Joseph Duffy, *Patrick in His Own Words*. © 1985 First published by Veritas Publications, Dublin. Used with permission.

33. From Michael Mitton, *The Soul of Celtic Spirituality: In the Lives of Its Saints*. Twenty-Third Publications, 1996. Used by permission. See also readings 79–80, and 116.

34–35. From John J. O'Meara, *The Voyage of Saint Brendan "Journey to the Promised Land."* Colin Smythe Ltd., 1991. Used by permission.

42–46. *The Celtic Monk: Rules & Writings of Early Irish Monks*. Translated and annotated by Uinseann Ó Maidín, Cistercian Publications, Kalamazoo, Michigan, 1996. Used by permission. See also readings 64-68, 73-74, 82-85, 114.

49. From *Iona: The Earliest Poetry of a Celtic Monastery* by Thomas Owen Clancy and Gilbert Markus. Edinburgh University Press, 1995. Used by permission. See also readings 52–53, 56, 59-61, 63, 69-72.

54. From *In Search of Columba* by Lesley Whiteside. Blackrock, Co. Dublin: Columba Press, 1997. Used by permission.

78. "From Erin's Shores" in *Love From Below*. Wild Goose Resource Group, Wild Goose Publications/The Iona Community, Glasgow, 1992.

81. From John J. Ó Ríordáin, *The Music of What Happens*. Blackrock, Co. Dublin: Columba Press, 1996. Used by permission.

91–102. From Tomás Ó Fiaich. *Columbanus in His Own Words*. © Veritas Publications, Dublin. Used with permission.

RESOURCES

Adam, David. *The Cry of the Deer: Meditations on the Hymn of St. Patrick.* Harrisburg, Penn.: Morehouse, 1987.

___. *The Edge of Glory: Prayers in the Celtic Tradition.* Wilton, Conn.: Morehouse-Barlow, 1985.

___. *The Wisdom of the Celts.* Grand Rapids, Mich.: Eerdmans, 1996.

Adomnan of Iona. *Life of St. Columba.* Translated by Richard Sharpe. London: Penguin, 1995.

The Age of Bede. Translated by J.F. Webb. Edited with an introduction by D.H. Farmer. London: Penguin, 1998.

Allchin, A.M., and Esther de Waal, eds. *Daily Readings from Prayers & Praises in the Celtic Tradition.* Springfield, Ill.: Templegate, 1987.

Anderson, Mosa. *St. Ninian: Light of the Celtic North.* London: Faith Press, 1964.

Backhouse, Janet. *The Lindisfarne Gospels: A Masterpiece of Book Painting.* London: British Library, 1995.

Baring-Gould, S. *The Lives of the Saints.* Edinburgh: John Grant, 1914.

Bede. *The Ecclesiastical History of the English People.* Edited by Judith McClure and Roger Collins. New York: Oxford University Press, 1994.

Bernard, J. H., and R. Atkinson. *The Irish Liber Hymnorum.* London: Harry Bradshaw Society, 1898.

Bitel, Lisa M. *Isle of the Saints: Monastic Settlements and Christian Community in Early Ireland.* Ithaca, N.Y.: Cornell University Press, 1990.

Bradley, Ian. *Celtic Christianity: Making Myths and Chasing Dreams.* Edinburgh: Edinburgh University Press, 1999.

___. *The Celtic Way.* London: Darton, Longman, and Todd, 1995.

__. *Columba: Pilgrim and Penitent*. Glasgow: Wild Goose, 1996.

Brooks, Daphne. *Wild Men and Holy Places*. Edinburgh: Canongate, 1994.

Cahill, Thomas. *How the Irish Saved Civilization: The Untold Story of Ireland's Heroic Role from the Fall of Rome to the Rise of Medieval Europe.* New York: Bantam/Doubleday, 1995.

Carmichael, Alexander, ed. *Carmina Gadelica: Hymns and Incantations*. 2 vols. Edinburgh: T. and A. Constable, 1900.

Carney, James. *Mediaeval Irish Lyrics*. Dublin: Dolmen, 1967; Berkeley, Calif.: University of California Press, 1967.

__. *Early Irish Poetry*. Cork: Mercier, 1965.

Clancy, Thomas, and Gilbert Markus. *Iona: The Earliest Poetry of a Celtic Monastery.* Edinburgh: Edinburgh University Press, 1995.

Davies, Oliver, and Fiona Bowie, eds. *Celtic Christian Spirituality: An Anthology of Medieval and Modern Sources.* New York: Continuum, 1995.

de Paor, Liam. *St. Patrick's World: The Christian Culture of Ireland's Apostolic Age.* Notre Dame, Ind.: University of Notre Dame Press, 1993.

de Waal, Esther, ed. *The Celtic Vision: Prayers and Blessings from the Outer Hebrides. Selections from the Carmina Gadelica.* Petersham, Mass.: St. Bede, 1988.

__. *The Celtic Way of Prayer: The Recovery of the Religious Imagination.* New York: Doubleday, 1997.

__. *Every Earthly Blessing: Rediscovering the Celtic Tradition. Celebrating a Spirituality of Creation.* Ann Arbor, Mich.: Servant, 1992.

Duffy, Joseph. *Patrick in His Own Words*. Dublin: Veritas, 1985.

Finlay, Ian. *Columba*. London: Victor Gollancz, 1979.

Flower, Robin. *The Irish Tradition*. Oxford: Clarendon, 1948.

__. *The Western Island*. London: Oxford University Press, 1978.

Forbes, Alexander Penrose, ed. *Lives of St. Ninian and St. Kentigern.* Edinburgh: Edmonston and Douglas, 1874.

Gill, Elaine, and Courtney Davis. *The Book of Celtic Saints*. London: Blandford, 1995.

Graves, Alfred Perceval, ed. *The Book of Irish Poetry*. Dublin: Talbot Press, n.d.

__. *A Celtic Psaltery*. London: SPCK, 1917.

Hanson, R.P.C. *The Life and Writings of the Historical Saint Patrick*. New York: Seabury, 1983.

Heaney, Seamus. *Station Island*. New York: Farrar, Straus, Giroux, 1985.

Hull, Eleanor, ed. *The Poem Book of the Gael*. London: Chatto and Windus, 1912.

Jackson, Kenneth, ed. *A Celtic Miscellany: Translations from the Celtic Literatures*. London: Routledge & Kegan Paul, 1951.

Joyce, Timothy. *Celtic Christianity: A Sacred Tradition, A Vision of Hope*. Maryknoll, N.Y.: Orbis, 1998.

Kennelly, Brendan, ed. *The Penguin Book of Irish Verse*. Middlesex: Penguin, 1981.

Lacey, Brian. *Colum Cille and the Columban Tradition*. Dublin: Four Courts, 1997.

Macdonald, Ian, ed. *St. Brendan*. Edinburgh: Floris, 1992.

__, **ed.** *St. Columba*. Edinburgh: Floris, 1992.

__, **ed.** *St. Patrick*. Edinburgh: Floris, 1992.

__, **ed.** *St. Margaret*. Edinburgh: Floris, 1993.

__, **ed.** *St. Mungo*. Edinburgh: Floris, 1993.

__, **ed.** *St. Ninian*. Edinburgh: Floris, 1993.

__, **ed.** *Saints of Northumbria: Cuthbert, Aidan, Oswald, Hilda*. Edinburgh: Floris, 1997.

Mackey, James, ed. *An Introduction to Celtic Christianity*. Edinburgh: T & T Clark, 1989.

Maclean, Magnus. *The Literature of the Celts: Its History and Romance*. London: Blackie and Son, 1902.

MacQueen, John. *St. Nynia*. Edinburgh: Polygon, 1990.

Marsden, John. *The Illustrated Life of Columba*. Edinburgh: Floris, 1995.

__. *Sea-Road of the Saints: Celtic Holy Men in the Hebrides*. Edinburgh: Floris, 1995.

Matthews, Caitlin. *The Celtic Spirit: Daily Meditations for the Turning Year*. San Francisco: Harper San Francisco, 1999.

Meehan, Bernard. *The Book of Kells.* London: Thames and Hudson, 1996.

Meyer, Kuno. *Selections from Ancient Irish Poetry.* London: Constable & Co., 1911.

Mitton, Michael. *The Soul of Celtic Spirituality: In the Lives of Its Saints.* Mystic, Conn.: Twenty-Third, 1996.

Moorhouse, Geoffrey. *Sun Dancing: A Vision of Medieval Ireland.* New York: Harcourt Brace & Company, 1997.

Murphy, Gerard, ed. *Early Irish Lyrics: Eighth to Twelfth Century.* Oxford: Clarendon, 1956.

Newell, J. Philip. *Celtic Prayers from Iona.* New York: Paulist, 1997.

__. *Listening for the Heartbeat of God: A Celtic Spirituality.* New York: Paulist, 1997.

O Clery, Michael, comp. *The Martyrology of Donegal: A Calendar of the Saints of Ireland.* Translated by John O'Donovan. Edited by James Henthorn Todd and William Reeves. Dublin: Irish Archaeological and Celtic Society, 1864.

O'Donohue, John. *Anam Cara: A Book of Celtic Wisdom.* New York: Cliff Street Books/HarperCollins, 1997.

__. *Eternal Echoes: Exploring Our Yearning to Belong.* New York: Cliff Street Books/HarperCollins, 1999.

O'Donoghue, Denis. *Brendaniana: St. Brendan the Voyager.* Dublin: Browne & Nolan, 1895.

Ó Fiaich, Tomás Cardinal. *Columbanus in His Own Words.* Dublin: Veritas, 1990.

O'Hanlon, John. *Lives of the Irish Saints.* Dublin: James Duffy & Sons, 1891.

O'Kelleher, A., and G. Schoepperle. *Betha Colaim Chille: Life of Columcille.* Urbana, Ill.: University of Illinois Press, 1918.

Ó Maidín, Uinseann, trans. *The Celtic Monk: Rules and Writings of Early Irish Monks.* Kalamazoo, Mich.: Cistercian, 1996.

O'Meara, John J. *The Voyage of Saint Brendan: "Journey to the Promised Land."* Translated from the Latin. Gerrards Cross, Buckinghamshire: Colin Smythe Limited, 1991.

Ó Ríordáin, John J. *The Music of What Happens: Celtic Spirituality. A View from the Inside*. Winona, Minn.: Saint Mary's Press, 1996.

__. *A Pilgrim in Celtic Scotland*. Dublin: Columba, 1997.

Pennick, Nigel. *The Celtic Saints: An Illustrated and Authoritative Guide to These Extraordinary Men and Women*. New York: Sterling, 1997.

__. *The Sacred World of the Celts: An Illustrated Guide to Celtic Spirituality and Mythology*. Rochester, Vt.: Inner Traditions International, 1997.

Plummer, Charles. *Lives of Irish Saints*. Oxford: Clarendon, 1922.

Rabey, Steve. *In the House of Memory: Ancient Celtic Wisdom for Everyday Life*. New York: Dutton, 1998.

Rodgers, Michael, and Marcus Losack. *Glendalough: A Celtic Pilgrimage*. Harrisburg, Penn.: Morehouse, 1996.

Roy, Charles. *Islands of Storm*. Chester Springs, Penn.: Dufour Editions, 1991.

Sellner, Edward S. *Wisdom of the Celtic Saints*. South Bend, Ind.: Ave Maria, 1993.

Sheldrake, Philip. *Living Between Worlds: Place and Journey in Celtic Spirituality*. Boston: Cowley, 1995.

Simpson, Ray. *Celtic Blessings: Prayers for Everyday Life*. Chicago: Loyola, 1999.

__. *Exploring Celtic Spirituality*. London: Hodder and Stoughton, 1995.

Skinner, John, trans. *The Confession of Saint Patrick*. New York: Image, 1998.

Stevenson, Rev. William. *The Legends and Commemorative Celebrations of St. Kentigern, His Friends, and Disciples*. Translated from the Aberdeen Breviary and the Arbuthnott Missal. Edinburgh: Thomas George Stevenson, 1872.

Stokes, Whitley. *The Martyrology of Oengus the Culdee*. London: Henry Bradshaw Society, 1905.

Stone, Samuel. *Lays of Iona and Other Poems*. London: Longmans, Green, 1897.

Taylor, Thomas. *The Celtic Christianity of Cornwall*. London: Longmans Green, 1956.

Thurston, Herbert, and Donald Attwater, eds. *Butler's Lives of the Saints*.

Westminster, Md.: Christian Classics, 1956.

Toulson, Shirley. *The Celtic Year: A Month by Month Celebration of Celtic Christian Festivals and Sites.* Rockport, Mass.: Element, 1993.

Van de Weyer, Robert. *Celtic Prayers: A Book of Celtic Devotion, Daily Prayers, and Blessings.* Dublin: Gill & Macmillan, 1997.

Wallace, Martin. *Celtic Saints.* San Francisco: Chronicle, 1995.

Watts, Murray. *The Wisdom of Saint Columba of Iona.* Oxford: Lions, 1997.

Whiteside, Lesley. *In Search of Columba.* Dublin: Columba, 1997.

__. *The Spirituality of St. Patrick.* Harrisburg, Penn.: Morehouse, 1996.